Walter Arnold

Money and Banking

A lecture delivered at the Mechanics' Institute, Toronto

Walter Arnold

Money and Banking
A lecture delivered at the Mechanics' Institute, Toronto

ISBN/EAN: 9783744795579

Printed in Europe, USA, Canada, Australia, Japan

Cover: Foto ©Suzi / pixelio.de

More available books at **www.hansebooks.com**

MONEY & BANKING;

A LECTURE

DELIVERED AT THE

MECHANICS' INSTITUTE, TORONTO,

Exposing the swindling nature of the present Banking System, and shewing how most of the failures that occur are caused by that system ; shewing also how an Inconvertible or Domes'ic Currency could protect and stimulate the Industry of the Country ; how unjust and monstrously expensive for raising Revenue the Tariff System is, compared with Direct Taxation, and how the country can at once be relieved of the greater portion of its Public Debt.

~~~~~~~~~~~~~~~~~~~~~~

To the above has been added some further remarks on Bank-debt as currency, as well as a definition of Protection.

BY WALTER ARNOLD, ESQ.,

BARRISTER-AT-LAW.

~~~~~~~~~~~~~~~~~~~~

"The functions of money are so interwoven with the affairs of men that its stability and uniformity of value are almost as essential to their prosperity as is the establishment and maintenance of the right of property itself."—OPDYKE's POL. EC.

———◆———

TORONTO:

BLACKBURN'S CITY STEAM PRESS, YONGE STREET.

1861.

MONEY AND BANKING.

GENTLEMEN :—

Monetary science has been rendered complicated by
reason of the confused notions of writers on the subject.
Its principles are few and simple, and, I trust, I shall be
able so to present them, that you will readily comprehend
them. When you do so, I may safely reckon on your
assistance to overthrow the present Banking System; than
which a better system could not be devised to retard the
material and social progress of the country.

I shall first distinguish between the resources and the
wealth of a country. I will then explain what is Currency;
what is Money; and what is the Measure of Value. I will shew
how the Measure of Value can be affected; and how it is
affected by the present Banking system. I will then explain
the meaning of Capital, to prove the fallacy of the theory
in currency termed Lawism. When you thoroughly understand these several matters. you will be familiar with the
fundamental principles of monetary science, and by them
can test the soundness or fallacy of any currency scheme
presented to your notice.

The Resources of a country are all those objects which,
taken by themselves, are not wealth, but which are capable
of being applied to the production of wealth. They comprehend, in the first instance, the objects upon which industry may be usefully employed; such as fertile soils, minerals,
forests, &c.; secondly, the fund of industry which may be
employed upon them; and, thirdly, the power which puts

that industry in motion, which is *Money*. None of these, taken singly, can be of any use, but a judicious combination of the whole produces wealth. Wealth is the production of useful industry, objects capable of ministering to the wants and tastes of mankind ; and Resources are the materials, or means applicable to such purpose. Money is more properly to be regarded as one of the resources of the nation, rather than part of its actual wealth, because though industry has been bestowed on its production, yet its production is only a means to an end, and not the end itself.

The use of money is to set industry in motion ; but what is money ? Before defining it I will explain the meaning of currency. We will suppose there be three persons, respectively named A, B, C ; A performs services for B, and at the time does not require B's services ; B then becomes indebted to A, and gives him some token or acknowledgment of the debt. A writing to that effect would be sufficient. A afterwards requires C's services, C wants not A's, but wishes for B's. What more natural than for A to transfer B's obligation to C, who readily accepts it, well knowing B's capability of fulfilling his promise   C then transfers B's obligation to some one else, and so this written obligation or evidence of debt, would pass from hand to hand, or be current, and from the use of it the thing itself would be what is called a *Currency*.

This simple consideration at once shews the nature of a currency ; that its use is to facilitate the transference of debt from one person to another ; and that whatever means be adopted for that purpose, whether it be gold, silver, or paper, is a currency.

Currency, then, is nothing more than the evidence of services having been rendered, for which an equivalent has not been received, but which can at any time be demanded. We may, therefore lay down that *Currency* and *Transferable Debt* are *Convertable Terms;* whatever represents transferable debt is *currency*, and whatever material the currency may consist of represents *transferable debt,* and nothing else.

When a person receives an obligation expressed by a metallic currency, he is able to command the services not only of the original debtor, but also those of the whole industrious community. The general consent of the whole nation, or of any number of nations, to receive the metallic currency in return for services, does not in any way alter its nature, nor could it have any value beyond those countries Consequently it would perform the same functions as the paper currency above mentioned, but it would have a *much wider circulation.*

There is clearly no difference in principle between a metallic and a paper currency, only one depends on a *wider basis of credit,* than the other. A metallic currency is subject to its own peculiar disadvantages, because by its constant wear and tear, as it passes from hand to hand, it suffers considerably by abrasion, not to mention any bad practices that may be resorted to to lessen its weight ; and as the quantity or weight of the metal represents the amount of the services the owner may command, as the metal decreases in weight, so does the amount of the service it represents and can command gradually and correspondingly diminish. Paper is not subject to this intrinsic depreciation, so that if it were possible to have a paper currency based *upon the same credit,* and which would be *as generally received* as the metallic currency, it would be a preferable form.

The amount of currency in a country is the aggregate amount of it belonging to every individual. Now whatever represents the amount of debt due to any individual, in whatever form that debt be recorded, whether metal or paper, or whether it exists simply as a debt, is the amount of the currency belonging to him. Whatever, therefore, confers the power of demanding services, or professes to confer the power of demanding them, is the currency or circulating medium of any single person ; and includes not only the current money of the realm, but whatever represents or displaces it. Adopting this definition we may enumerate the different species of currency as follows :

1. Coined money. Gold, silver and copper.

2. Bills of exchange, including cheques.
3. Promisory notes, including bank notes.
4. The sum standing at his credit in his banker's books.
5. Private debts.

The sum standing at his credit in his banker's books is clearly a portion of a man's circulating medium ; and is to be considered very much in the same light as the paper circulation of the bank ; because he can at any moment convert them into a cheque, which is a bill of exchange, payable to bearer on demand, and is in all respects equivalent to a bank note. Bank notes, as is well known, are nothing more, but *promisory notes* of the banks, *payable to bearer on demand.* No writer ever hesitated to admit that bank notes are essentially part of the currency of the country ; many regulations have been made restricting their issues. But banks have also *bills of exchange payable to bearer on demand,* though as they are the *acceptors* of these, they of course, do not issue them.   These bills are most commonly known by the name of *cheques,* and they in no way differ from bills of exchange.

The great and important portion of the currency which consists of cheques has not been sufficiently appreciated. The attention of speakers, writers and legislators on the *paper currency* has been almost exclusively directed to bank notes ; whereas all the ideas involved in bank notes are, with a small change in the form of expression, applicable to cheques ; and there is no operation whatever which a bank can promote by means of bank notes, which it cannot, with equal efficacy, perform by means of cheques. If it wishes to advance a speculation instead of giving its customer so many of its promisory notes, it promises to honor his cheques to an equal amount.

It is often said that no London banker issues notes ; and hence it is too often hastily concluded that no London bank but the Bank of England deals in paper currency.   But it is impossible to conceive a greater fallacy than this.   Formerly the London banks all issued notes, or deposit receipts, which before the stamp laws were transferrable by delivery.

About seventy years ago, they dropped the practice of issuing notes directly themselves, and adopted one which was far more secure for themselves. They gave each of their customers a book containing a number of blank acceptances, which he might fill up and issue at his convenience, and these were called cheques. This system prevails at present, and is the very foundation of London Banking. " Whatever effects the issuing of bank notes has upon specutors or prices, or in driving gold out of circulation, is equally effectually done by cheques and the inevitable tendency of a *perfect banking system* is to *drive gold out of circulation* and *to substitute paper for it* " So says McLeod in his " Theory and Practice of Banking ; " and this is perfectly true, the present banking system drives the money out of the country, and Bank debt occupies its place.

The deposits are the largest portion of the currency of the country. They constitute the medium of exchange of all the large transactions of commerce. They comprise the "money," so called, of the merchants and manufacturers. It is their increase or decrease which causes prices to rise and fall. The variation in the amount of notes in circulation is comparatively limited, but in the amount of deposits is great and frequent.

Private debts are also a portion of a man's circulating medium, in the same way as the figures at his credit in his banker's books ; for they can be converted into a bill of exchange at the pleasure of the parties ; nor does a debt due from a private person differ from one due from a banker, except perhaps in security. It is certainly true that some of these descriptions of currency are more eligible and secure than others, but they are all essentially of the same nature and perform the same duties with different degrees of advantage. The metallic currency rests upon its own intrinsic value and the credit of the State that it is of the proper weight and fineness.

Among the different species of currency I have named coins, gold, silver and copper ; they are Money, and are distinguished from the other currencies by being *that currency which* government makes *a legal tender in payment of debts.*

This legal tender at different periods and in different nations has been composed of a variety of substances; at present in most nations it is composed of certain metals, which have received an impress from the Sovereign power of the State. They are then called coins, and are Money in the country that issues them, but not so in any other country, except where special provision is made to receive them as such. In foreign countries coins are merely bullion, and receive the same consideration as any other commodity of commerce.

The simplest and most perfect form of Money is that which represents *nothing but transferable debt* and of which the material is of *no intrinsic value*, such as paper. It is only, however, when States have reached a high degree of civilization that they will adopt, under proper regulations, this most perfect form. At present the material of it consists of something which has an intrinsic value, such as gold and silver. From this circumstance the purchase of an article with a gold coin is of a mixed character, and partakes somewhat of the nature both of a barter and a sale. But the *intrinsic value* is of a *secondary consideration* and not the one which gives it its characteristic of money. It is its general reception as the visible symbol of transferable debt, which constitutes the essence of money, and distinguishes a coin from a similar piece of metal of another shape.

The difference between conducting commercial transactions by way of barter and by means of the intervention of money, is that in the former case, they are considered directly as *equivalents*, in the latter they proceed in the tacit assumption of the geometrical axiom that things which are *equal to the same* are *equal to each other*. Money is that third thing which is used as the common measure, to which every thing else is referred, and the superiority of the latter method of conducting commerce is so obvious and decided that it has universally superseded the former among civilized nations.

When there is much money in a country, the prices of property and services are high; when there is little prices are low. It is therefore the amount of money in a country that regulates the price of property and services, and thus it is that money becomes the Measure of Value. It is essential to the character of whatever is used as money that it be liable as little as possible to fluctuation in quantity. The reason is obvious. He who contracted debts when money bore one ratio to products would pay them when it bore another ratio; and hence, though he might pay the same nominal amount, yet he might pay twice as much in value as he had promised. So also, he who loaned money, while it bore one ratio, and received his payments while it was at another, though he might receive the same nominal amount, might not receive half the amount in value which he loaned. And hence all civilized nations have denied to governments for the purpose of making more money, the right of altering. or in any manner interfering with the right or purity of coin, for the reason that this causes a variation in the quantity of money, and thus interferes with private contracts.

Were tampering with the coin allowed, it is evident that credit must be at an end, because whatever a contract might mean to-day, no one could possibly predict what it would mean to-morrow. Hence, all fluctuation in the quantity of any substance, renders it by the amount of that fluctuation, unfit for the purposes of money.

Now these remarks apply to anything which may be used as money. They apply to silver and gold; if these substances were liable to great fluctuations in quantity we should be obliged to abandon them and find something better; and it is the same with paper, if it were used for money purposes; by as much as it is liable to sudden or to great fluctuations in quantity, by so much is it disserviceable for the purposes of money.

In order to accomplish a given number of exchanges in a community, a certain amount of money is necessary, and no more than this is necessary for this purpose. If to accomplish the exchanges of a community at a given time, one thousand ounces of silver are necessary, and twice the quantity be introduced, to accomplish the exchanges the value of the whole will remain the same, though the quantity varies, and the result will be, that the value of money in relation to other products will fall one half; that is, if we gave five dollars for a hat before, we shall give ten dollars now, and for other things in proportion. And if half of the one thousand ounces were removed the reverse would be the case, that is, the value of money would be doubled; in other words, if we gave five dollars for a hat formerly, we should give $2\frac{1}{2}$ now, and so of other productions.

The metallic currency of a nation, in consequence of its general utility in the commercial world, and the impossibility of obtaining it in sufficiently large quantities, is not liable to great fluctuations within short periods. But the quantity of paper in circulation depends very much on the interest of its issuers. Hence the quantity may vary in almost any amount, and as the value of the whole is not altered by the quantity in use, as the quantity increases the value of each portion must decrease; and hence a paper dollar may be worth twenty-five per cent more or less to-day than it was a month ago. Though there be the same words written upon the paper, and it be called by the same name, yet it means to him that pays it and to him who receives it, a very different thing from what it did a month ago. He bought, three months ago, a thousand barrels of flour at ten dollars a barrel, at three months. Without any change in the supply or the demand for flour, he is not now able to sell it for more than seven dollars a barrel, while his note for ten thousand dollars must be paid in full.

The paper currency under the present banking system is liable to these sudden and great fluctuations, and the manner in which this occurs is easily explained.

Suppose that at a given period, the circulating medium in a community is perfectly proportioned to the necessities of exchange, and that the medium, though paper, is perfectly sound; that is, that there exists in all the banks, sufficient specie to pay all liabilties of the banks on demand in the precious metals.

Let now from any cause whatever, the productiveness of

labor be greatly increased, so that a much larger amount of products is brought into market. If the amount of money remains the *same*, while the amount of products is *increased*, the value of money will rise, that is, every thing will be cheap. As soon as products become cheap, every one is anxious to buy, for when an article is low in any country then is the time to export it with advantage; and this prospect will induce men to borrow to export, in the expectation that the profit will enable them to realize far more than the interest they have paid for borrowed capital. At such a time every one is desirous of borrowing; and banks thinking they can profitably employ their funds, loan to the utmost extent of their power, instigated by their own interests, and by the universal wish of the public.

Now in such a state of things it is not to be supposed that the Directors of Banks are endowed with greater prudence than other men, or that they are not as likely to be influenced by the hope of large dividends. The example of one stimulates the others, the risk that one institution runs, another will be willing to run. A bank will scarcely be willing to make a dividend of six per cent, whilst its neighbour is making eight. And when all the Banks in the country are animated by these principles, it is evident that a very large amount of loans must be effected; that is, a very large amount of paper currency, in *ledger credits* and *bank notes*, must be created. But just as fast as beyond the necessary amount, the quantity is increased, the value of each portion diminishes, and thus prices rise; that is, money becomes abundant, and a dollar will purchase no more than it would when products were scarce. Thus, the amount of circulating medium becomes very great, and *Money* is *cheaper than any other article in the market.*

The cheapest article in the market will always be exported; as this is now money, money will be exported, and as the bills are worth nothing abroad, they will be collected and sent into the banks for redemption. The banks then find themselves liable to pay in specie a vastly greater amount than they were liable to pay a short time ago and the demand for specie increases. They are of course in danger of stopping payment, and their only means of safety is in diminishing their loans, that is, loaning no more and requiring payment of those who owe them. Hence, those who had borrowed with the hopes of paying by means of their sales, are called upon to pay before their sales are effected ; and as the banks refuse to loan very few are disposed to buy. The debtors of the banks are required to pay their debts sooner than they expected, and the means of making those payments are curtailed. The money goes into the banks and but little comes out. Every day the quantity of circulating medium is diminished, the scarcity of money increases, the price of goods falls, as men will sell for lower. and lower prices, rather than lose their credit. Every man from necessity presses his neighbour and the banks from the same necessity presses them all. And thus, in a few months the amount of circulating medium is greatly diminished, and money is worth 25 or 50 per cent. more than it was a short time ago. He who agreed to pay 1000 ounces of silver when one ounce of silver was worth a bushel of wheat, pays it now, when it is worth one bushel and a half of wheat, that is, though he pays the same nominal amount, he pays 50 per cent. more in value.

Sometimes the pressure for money is so great that those who have purchased products with borrowed capital, cannot sell them fast enough to make their payments. They are obliged to stop payments, or become bankrupts and assign their effects to their creditors. But these were debtors to many others, who were depending on the payment to be received from them, to pay their own debts. These being disappointed also fail. Their failure leads again to the failure of others, and the panic becomes general. No one dares trust his neighbour and the banks dare not trust any one. An universal crash of mercantile credit succeds, and none are able to withstand the shock, save those of the heaviest capital and of the greatest financial ability.

When all this happens, things in the following way become re-established ; when a debtor fails, he assigns his property to his creditors, this being done his need of money is over and by so much diminishes the demand. His property is sold at any price it will bring, this depressing still more rapidly the price of goods and raising the comparative value of money will cause specie to be rapidly imported. As soon as these causes have had time to operate, that is diminished demand and increased· supply, the equilibirum is restored and credit is established on its ordinary basis.

Here you have an exemplification of the workings of the present banking system and as a Mixed Currency, that is, a mixture of specie and bank-paper, forms the measure of value in every country in which it circulates, as truly as a specie currency, you see by these expansions and contractions of the banks how the measure of value must necessarily be affected. The error and pernicious principle of our banking system may be rendered still plainer by the following illustration.

There is one Koh-i-noor diamond in the world and only one. What if we create a corporation to deal in Koh-i-noor diamonds, the one being put in for capital with authority to issue ten different promises to deliver the diamond on demand. So long as the diamond remains on deposit, and people are satisfied that they can get it by presenting the certificate of claim, the certificate may pass and command an equivalent in commodities; and the promise to pay the diamond can be readily discharged, or more properly evaded, by presenting another promise against it of the same sort. All these promises make good "deposits." A checks upon the corporation for a diamond and is paid in its promise., The "Grand Confidence" of the public will thus make the community worth apparently ten Koh-i-noor diamonds while they and the world possess but one; and that same confidence will *pay interest* in cloth, corn, wine, and other good things to the diamond corporation for their *sound currency* as *good as diamonds.* But then somebody discovers that where diamonds are so plenty, the equivalent in commodities is much smaller than in London. He pays the equivalent for one of the diamond promises, walks into the office of the corporation

B

and walks out with the gem. Another hearing of the good report of the London market walks in with another of these promises. The Teller hands out a new promise for the old one. "But Mr. Teller, I want the diamond." "Well I give you our promise which is just as good, it commands the *equivalent* in market, anybody will take it for dry-goods, or hardware, or software." " Perhaps so, but I happen to want nothing drier, or harder, or softer than a Koh-i-noor diamond, I have the promise of your corporation for the *specific thing* and know no *equivalent*, you will please hand out the diamond." At this point of the negociation, the teller probably puts his finger to his eye and lifting up the lid replies; " Do you see anything green under there'?" This reply is no invention, as it was once made by a teller of a bank out west, and may be considered the improved western method of declaring a crisis.

Here is a suspension, what follows; the corporation has taken care to loan its promises to substantial persons only, who have given their promises to pay a diamond in return. They are called upon to discharge their promises, but the thing required for doing so is not in the country. Their property consequently falls into the hands of the Sheriff, and the lucky man who, in the mean time, obtains the thing from abroad buys at his own price, and in this way are many ruined.

You will perhaps think this procedure of the diamond corporation swindling. There is no *perhaps* in the matter. It *is* swindling, and to just such swindling is committed, the vast business of the country, the hopes and aims of men, the happiness of families and all the material purposes of life. It is precisely as impossible to discharge with one dollar obligations to pay ten dollars, as to discharge with one diamond obligations to pay ten diamonds. If any one gets possession of one of these promises and demands the thing itself, and withdraws it from circulation, then there is a crisis.

If the diamond corporation had loaned the only one dia-

'mond they possessed, instead of promises to pay nine more
than nobody possessed, there would have been no crisis, no
impossibility in their contract and none in the contracts
depending upon it, because the diamond, or the certificate
for it, would have passed in each transfer and would repass
back to the original lender, the corporation, who would then
obtain the diamond, or their certificate for it, if they had
loaned the certificate instead of the diamond itself. This is
all that we need or anybody needs that if we buy or borrow
from the bank, we want the thing we buy or borrow as from
an individual; and if we take a certificate or a credit from
it, the Bank must hold the thing until the return of the
certificate or presentation of our check as ours, and subject
to our order, precisely as a wharfinger would hold wheat or
beef on storage, as the property of the buyer after he sold
it; the certificate would pass fifty times from hand to hand
without embarrassing any body. As it is the banks pledge
the same coin several times and when called upon it to pay
it, they have only promises of debtors to pay the demand,
then they demand of their debtors a thing they never loaned
and their debtors have only promises from their debtors
wherewith to respond. Of course there is a difficulty. The
banks may screw the thing from their debtors, so long as
the debtors can obtain it by any *sacrifice* of their property;
but beyond this there are dollars that cannot be paid.
because they never existed.

It is a common error even among bankers to suppose that
they always discount on their deposits, that is to say, on
previously existing funds, whereas the discount creates the
deposit; and the only question the banks consider is
whether the reserve of coin is sufficient to meet returning
liabilities. Thus, Smith purchases goods to the amount of
$10,000 and gives his note for the same. Smith's creditors
gets his note discounted at the bank and have say $10,000,
placed to their credit as "money deposited." If the bank
transferred that amount of money to their credit, it would
be a *real deposit* and the transaction would be perfectly
legitimate and proper; the bank would *transfer* and not
create a deposit. It would do what it is now supposed to

do, namely loan pre-existing fuuds ; but now it does not do this, but inscribes a ledger credit called " deposit." Next, Smith sells his goods, takes his customers' notes, gets them discounted and has $10,000 placed to his credit as " money deposited." We may suppose this thing to be again repeated another $10,000 being created in the favor of the third seller of the same goods. Here is then $30,000 of currency created, having all the *purchasing power of gold coin.*

This fictitious currency is most mischeivous, and interferes as effectually with the value of money as would an undetected counterfeit currency whether of metal or paper : and when its nature is understood by the leading minds of the country, it will be as vigorously suppressed as base coin.

I trust from what has been advanced that it is clearly seen that when the Measure of Value, that is, the aggregate amount of money in a country, is constantly varying in amount, at one time greatly increased in volume, at another greatly reduced, how seriously must be affected the price of property, that is its value ; and how seriously must be affected those, who have liabilities, when a great reduction in the volume of the currency takes place. And you will better appreciate the effects of these fluctuations when, you consider that according to the results of investigations by some of the ablest statisticians of the United States, the money in proportion to the property in the United States is as 1 to 25 and in proportion to the circulating portion of that property as 1 to 10. So that every dollar of the currency circulates ten of property.

In estimating the power of currency to increase prices, we will assume for the sake of argument $30,000,000 as the sum of the currency and the circulating property estimated at $3)0,000,000 ; then if we double the currency without increasing the property the price of tne property increases to $6(0,0)0,000. Let any one reflect upon this and he will see why it is the precious metals are parted with. Every dollar added to the currency, whether in gold or bank debt, adds 10 dollars of price to our commodities in the aggregate. Assuming the whole sum of our currency to be $30,000,000 and our values level with Europe, so that the commodities we produce the more advantageously go to Europe and those Europeans produce more advantageously come here in a normal, wholesome traffic ; then let the $5,000,000 of currency be added and it will add $50,000,000 to our prices : our prices being raised will cause increased activity in the imports : and as our commodities have risen in price many that were before exportable cannot now be exported, consequently to pay for the imports money has to be exported, and will be exported till our prices are on a level with those of other countries. When these $5,000,000 of currency are bank debt the money leaves the country and debt takes its place. Should $5,000,000, instead of being added, be withdrawn from circulation it throws $50,000,000 of property on the rest of the currency for circulation.

Saunders, in his Observations on the Currency, says, " The panic of 1822 was caused by the Bank reducing its discounts (most likely he means deposits) from £15,000,-000 to £3,000,000, in order to secure the convertibility of the bank note, and by the contraction of the Bank of England and local notes, from £48,000,000 to £26,000,000 ; thus, in less than three years, reducing the volume of the currency by £34,000,000 ! This was a gold panic, lessening the price of funded and landed properties, the stock of goods held by the mercantile and trading interests, and agricultural products, to the extent of some £200,000,000." Saunders makes no reference to the reduction of discounts on the part of the other banks of the country, no doubt, this reached a large amount,—adding very much to the above sum of £34,000,000. It is only very lately that English writers on money have discovered that the deposits of banks compose part of its circulation, as much so as the paper they issue.

I believe it was about this time that a person in England bought two estates, for one he paid £80,000 cash ; for the other he gave £70,000, £10,000 down and the balance secured by mortgage over both estates. By a Parliamentary measure the amount of currency was afterwards so greatly reduced, that it required the sale of both properties to pay off the mortgage; and this man and his family were ruined. Beggared by a Parliamentary measure, he stated his case and petitioned Parliament for relief, but as you may well conceive, it was impossible for them to entertain his petition.

As respects the United States, the deposits and notes in circulation of the banks after deducting the coin in the banks, on January 1st, 1857 amounted to $416,000,000; on January 1st, 1858, this was reduced $104,000,000; on January 1st, 1859, the currency was increased $100,000,000, and continued to increase till 1st May following, when a sharp contraction ensued, till by the middle of August $35,000,000 were withdrawn from circulation.

How painful it is to contemplate such a state of things. Here is a measure large at one time and small at another. How unjust to a commercial people! Failures are inevitable; and a bankruptcy law indispensable.

I have not the bank statistics of this country, and if I had I need not detain you with them, for in all probability we should find their expansions and contractions, in proportion to the population, very similar to those of the United States.

I will now explain the original meaning of Capital, as it will enable me the better to prove the falacy of a theory in currency, which has been termed Lawism, because John Law was the first to write a formal treatise on it, and had the opportunity of carrying it out on the most extensive scale.

When a man is born without hereditary possessions and has no property presented to him, there is but one method by which he can live, that is by personal services, or labor of some description either mental or bodily. When such a person has found some one else who stands in need of his services and employs them, he is entitled to some compensation, some reward or wages. The first necessities of the laborer are food, clothing, and shelter. His employer must give him these things either directly, or else he may give him something, which will enable him to procure them from some one else. That something which is not an equivalent itself, *but only the means of obtaining an equivalent,* is money. This latter method of rewarding services is that almost universally adopted among civilized nations.

Now when the laborer has received his wages in money, he has has not received an equivalent for his services, but only something which will enable him to get what he requires. The money therefore that he possesses is not *the equivalent* but it is the symbol or proof that he has rendered services for which he has *not yet received an equivalent.* The laborer does not receive the coin for its own sake; what use can the actual silver be to him? but because it is the generally recognized and accepted power of commanding what he wants. Now if the laborer spends all his money in buying commodities for use, it is clear that the end of the year he is in no better condition than he was in the beginning. There is nothing but the same weary round of toil before him. He must again enter on a similar round of labor and personal services, to earn again the means of subsistence, and so on all for his life.

But suppose that instead of spending all his earnings on commodities, he saves a portion of them, then his condition at the end of the year is better just by so much as he has saved; and that saving represents such portion of his services rendered for which he has not yet received an equivalent. And that saving is called *Capital.* Whether it be a cent or a dollar, that is the first germ of Capital and the more the laborer saves the more does his capital increase. *The fundamental idea therefore of Capital, is the store of accumulated labor which its owner has not yet spent in purchasing commodities.* It does not represent commodities in any way whatever, but only the power of its owner to purchase what he pleases, and it is manifest that it bears no definite relation whatever to commodities, because the quantity of capital the laborer accumulates is just the quantity which he refrains from spending. Such then is the fundamental idea of Capital, which it is essential to grasp and retain. Capital is nothing but a store of accumulated labor which has not yet been spent and it is necessary to have some material substance to *represent* and *measure* it, and that substance is money.

The primary, genuine, and exclusive meaning then of Capital, is the accumulated savings of labor and its symbol is money. The first meaning which every man in business attaches to the expression Capital is money. Thus a capitalist is a person who has a large stock of money at his disposal, to bring capital into a business is to bring *money* into the concern. When a man is said not to have sufficient capital to carry on a business, it means that he has not sufficient command of ready money.

Money is the acknowledged symbol of capital, that is of accumulated labor, and whenever any one possesses this and wants to buy commodities, it is always a struggle between the two parties how much of his former services, how much money, he shall part with, in order to obtain the commodities he requires.

I will not here allude to the other senses in which the term Capital is used, as they do not affect the subject under consideration.

The fallacious theory in currency, termed *Lawism*, is that *Money represents commodities, and that paper currency may be based upon commodities.* This delusion is deeply prevalent in the public mind of the present day, and probably there are few persons except those who have studied the true philosophical principles of monetary science, whose views are not deeply tainted with this infection. No man who does not thoroughly purge his mind of this noxious principle, can ever attain the slightest knowledge of true monetary science. *Money does not represent commodities it all, but only Capital, the accumulation of labor which has not yet been given for commodities.* Every man who thinks that there is any necessary relation between the quantity of money in a country and its commodities, is a *Lawist.* Take the case of a private individual. Is there any necessary relation between the quantity of money he retains and the quantity of commodities he purchases? The quantity of money he has is just the quantity of capital, of services due to him, which he has not yet parted with for something else. It is the quantity of power of purchasing commodities he has over and above what he has already expended.

In fact a moment's consideration will at once shew that the theory of basing a paper currency on commodities, involves the palpable contradiction in terms, *That we can buy commodities and also have the money as well.* When a man buys commodities with money, he gives either a portion of his own industry represented by that money, or a portion of some one else's industry, who gave him the money. But it is quite clear that *he cannot buy the commodities and keep his money as well.* The idea of basing paper currency upon commodities is just as wild and absurd as if England were to sell her cotton goods to America for coin, and then demand back her cotton goods. The only result of an attempt to base a currency thus must be tremendous convulsions and destruction of credit and all monetary contracts.

The most striking confirmation of the preceding remarks is afforded by the examples of the Mississippi scheme in France, the Ayr Bank in Scotland, the creation of the Assignats during the French revolution,—and the great monetary convulsions in America in 1837–'9.

Law originated the Assignats in France. These were notes issued by Government, based on real security. The issues when at their height were certainly not anything equal in amount to the value of the fee-simple of France expressed in silver money; and according to the predictions of Law and Mirabeau, it was a matter of impossibility that they should ever become depreciated ; and what was the result ? Even though the experiment was not carried out to its full extent, the value of the paper assignat fell to 1-30,000 part of its value in silver. Such was the inevitable consequence of basing a paper currency upon property or securities, and such it must ever be, because if such issues are once begun, there is no legitimate conclusion whatever, until all the property in the country are issued into notes.

In reference to America, that country was unhappily deeply bitten with the currency mania of basing issues of paper on " *securities.*" In most of the States the Legislature passed acts permitting any individual, or any banking associations, to issue notes to any amount upon depositing with a " public Comptroller" securities of equivalent value. These securities might be public stock, or mortgages upon improved, productive and unincumbered lands. Now as these " securities" remained the property of those who gave them, and they might appropriate the revenues from them as long as payment of the notes was not demanded from the comptroller, people saw that they might derive a profit from the security as well as from the currency which represented its value. There was accordingly a prodigious rush to deposit securities, an enormous issue of paper during the years 1834, '5, '6. The people of the Western States, with their pockets full of paper currency, gave very large orders for goods to the merchants of New York, Boston and Philadelphia, who duly executed them. The bills given for these purchases were payable in these eastern cities, and when the western debtors went to their own bankers for bills of exchange on these places in return for their own local currency, the bankers discovered that their home customers had bought more from the eastern cities than they had sold ; that they had already drawn on the east for every dollar which the east was indebted to them and could draw no more. The western merchants then sent their own currency notes to the eastern cities, in payment, but unfortunately for them, the merchants there had already paid all they owed to the west ; nobody in New

York or Philadelphia wanted western notes for ahy purpose; and nobody was disposed to travel several thousand
miles to request the cashiers of the Western States to pay
their notes, or in those States in which securities had been
given to require the comptroller to sell the pledged securities and give them the money produce. Moreover, every
one knew that it was in either case impossible to obtain the
amount in money ; for there was no currency in which the
pledged property, when sold, could have been paid, except
bank notes resting on securities or on the mere promise of
the banker. In the mean time the usual effects followed,
specie disappeared from circulation. The extended paper
issues led the Americans to order immense quantities of
goods from Europe, and prices being very high from the
bloated paper currency, they could send no goods in return
to pay for them. For some time they sent over a great
quantity of their stock, but this became superabundant,
and at last no one in Europe would buy it. It became
necessary then for them to pay their debts in specie, but
specie there was none. In 1837, all the banks in America
without exception, stopped payment. The general suspension began at New York on the 18th of May and spread
in every direction. This was the fourth grand experiment
of Lawism, pure and unadulterated on the most magnifi-
cent scale, and such was the result.

All ideas therefore of basing a paper currency upon property of any description is essentially erroneous ; and can
have no other possible termination, if only carried out to
their legitimate consequences than what happened in France
in 1720, and in America in 1836-9. There is a species of
property however, which from its being more nearly con-
founded with money in the public ideas, is supposed by
many persons, who would repudiate any imputation of being
disciples of Law, to be a sound basis for a paper currency.
This property is public stock. A very prevalent idea is
that all banks of issue should give security by purchasing
the public funds, and then deposit the stock with a government officer. What is this but rank Lawism ? The rule
that is good for one is good for all. If the public funds are

a proper basis for $1000 of paper currency, they must of necessity be a good basis to their whole extent. If one bank or banker is allowed to issue paper on the security of stock, every other must be permitted to do the same, until the whole funded debt of the country is coined into paper notes. The principles of basing a paper currency upon land and upon the public funds, are absolutely identical and equally vicious. To permit a man to *spend* his money in buying part of the public debt, and to *have* it as well in the form of notes, is as rank an absurdity as to permit him to spend it in land and also have it as notes. The only advantage one has over the other is that the funds are more easily convertible into money than land is.

If the principle of basing a paper currency on lands and public funds be condemned, what shall be said of the principle, that banks adopt, of issuing to an amount several times more than the coin in their vaults, paper based on the security of individual indebtedness; surely this is the wildest kind of Lawism.

It is hoped that the preceding remarks are absolutely conclusive as to the fundamental fallacy of Lawism of all forms and descriptions, by which we mean the theory of basing issues of paper on property, on commodities, on public or on private indebtedness.

I will conclude that you are now conversant with the fundamental principles of monetary science, that is, that Currency is debt, which is transferable; that Money is that currency, which government makes a legal tender in payment of debts; that the Measure of Value is the aggregate amount of money in a country; and that Lawism, that is, the basing issues of paper on property of any description is fallacious.

We will now revert to the resources of the country. What are they? We have a most fertile soil; extensive forests; a country especially rich in minerals; fisheries unsurpassed; and unlimited water power; for a fund of industry, to convert these to the purposes of man, a population of 2,750,000; and for the power to set this industry in motion money for the most part fictitious and a measure of value that is continually varying.

This fictitious currency and imperfect measure of value, I have shewn, arise from the prevailing banking system; a system, which from its inception, has done nothing but plundered the country; limited its agriculture and manufactures; cramped its trade (interchanges among its people); and its commerce (interchanges with foreigners); and which causes, it is said, 93 out of every 100 who engage in business, to fail once in their lives.

A commercial community like this requires something that will facilitate the transference of debt from one person to another; and something that will serve, with some degree of permanence, to measure the relative value of different kinds of property and service; that is, a sound currency, and a Measure of Value of the most perfect kind. . The proper regulation of the measure of value is of the highest importance to every member in a community, particularly to business men; and it ought to be one of the chief functions of Government to make it as perfect as it can possibly be rendered. This can best be effected by having the money in a country, regulated in amount; valueless out of the country; and by preventing the circulation of any other currency that would be regarded as money.

Eminent writers on money consider that a specie currency by itself surpasses any other as a sound currency, and as a measure of value; but with them I cannot concur. It is true that a specie currency cannot be increased with the same facility as a paper currency; but in consequence of its importation and exportation as a *commodity*, and its conversion into articles for domestic use, it is liable to considerable fluctuations in quantity, thereby altering the measure of value and the value of money. By the introduction of what should be jealously kept as a medium of exchange into channels from which its nature ought to exclude it; and by the attempt to make it perform merchantable functions, functions foreign to its nature, and for which it was never intended, the measure of value injuriously fluctuates and no longer becomes that comparatively sure and safe measure, which apart from such influences it might become.

But setting aside the fluctuations in its value there are two important reasons why the adoption of a specie currency by this country is extremely objectionable. It is the currency of other countries; and this circumstance, firstly, may so interrupt its trade as to occasion incalculable distress; secondly, it will place the value of services in this country on a footing with the value of services in those countries wherever it is a currency, allowance first being made for the cost of transport from the foreign country. The great error, therefore, of adopting a currency common to other countries is that, besides interfering with the trade of this country, it places socially, its laborers, artisans and members of the industrial classes, on an equality with the laborers, artisans and industrial classes of other communities.

For illustration's sake, we will suppose the wants of the people of Canada are supplied, with the exception of one farmer and one manufacturer. The farmer has 1,000 bushels of wheat and the manufacturer 1,000 yards of cloth for sale. The market price of the wheat is $1 a bushel, of the cloth $1 a yard. The farmer requires 1,000 yards of cloth and the manufacturer 1,000 bushels of wheat. The farmers and manufacturers of a foreign country having more wheat and cloth than are required by the members of their community, discover the wants of the farmer and manufacturer in Canada. They require none of the products of Canada, but will accept for their wheat and cloth specie, which is a representative of services in their own country. They bring their wheat and cloth into the country, and undersell the farmer and manufacturer. The result of this is, the farmer and manufacturer expend their capital, and because no market present itself, either domestic or foreign, in which they can sell their goods, they remain on their hands; the farmer and manufacturer become embarrassed: the farmer discontinues improvements, and the manufacturer closes his factory for a season.

All this might have been avoided had the circulating medium been one *valueless out of the country ;* the foreigner not finding any products to exchange for his goods, would never have brought them into the country, the farmer and manufacturer would have exchanged their goods through the circulating medium, would have kept their capital, and been enabled to have proceeded vigorously with their undertakings.

I will suppose that the foreigners, who brought the wheat and cloth, come from a nation whos epeople are of low standing and of few wants : a people contented with a bare subsistence, whose consumption is consequently small, and who may always have therefore a considerable surplus for exportation. The foriegners seeing they can undersell our producers, will bring in products from their country and not wanting anything but our specie, will undersell the producers in Canada, till by the withdrawal of specie, they increase the value of money so much that our producers are reduced to nearly the level of the prices of the foreigners, the only dif-· ference being the cost of transport from the foreign country. In other words, our workmen hitherto have been receiving one dollar a day this supplying them with many comforts. but the foreigners accustomed to live meagrely, are contented with half a dollar a day, and as the specie currency enables them to introduce their goods into the country, our producers are obliged to place their services in competition with the services of the foreigners, thereby dragging down the position of our producers to a level with that of the foreigners.

In 1845 it was estimated at a very low calculation, to avoid exaggeration, that the labor saving machines of England were equivalent to every laborer having under him *forty workmen* that required neither food nor clothing. Ought not then abundance to prevail there ? Instead of which, owing to England's vicious monetary and banking system her laborers but barely subsist. Shall we have a currency in common with

such a country ? And because our people will not work for the
pauper wages of England, shall we be merely tillers of the
soil, mere producers of the raw material ? Shall we have no
manufactories, except such as are maintained by heavily
taxing consumers ? Shall we in fact place the social position
of our industrial class on a footing with the industrial classes
of England ? Every one I am sure will say, not if we can
help it. Let us, then, have a currency of our own ; and let us
adopt the simplest and most perfect form that which represents nothing but transferable debt, and of which the material
is of no intrinsic value, such as paper.

On a small scale, we already have such a currency in our
Postage Stamps. These the Government issues on receiving
value in services. or its representative, money, and for them
promises to render services when returned to them on letters
or packages, passing through the post office. On account of
the services, Government is always ready to render for these
stamps, they have become a currency, and are readily received in payment of small sums, but this only in Canada, for
out of the country they are valueless.

Seeing how these stamps answer as a currency, the Government under proper restrictions, and on a fixed plan, might
issue paper on a much larger scale and convert it into money
by making it a legal tender.

As regards the limit of the issues of a paper currency, due
regard should be had to the trade and business habits of
a people, and an estimate should be made of the ratio that
the amount of the currency should bear to population. This
estimate once made, that ratio should always be observed ;
for as population increases business will also increase, and to
keep up the relation between money and capital, an enlarge-
ment of the currency should take place. I believe no better
plan can be adopted, by this means the currency would be
steady in amount, and fluctuations in its value would depend
only on a change in the ratio commodities bore to it. In a
normal condition of things, this would be continually increasing and the movement of the currency would be towards

a gradual increase in value ; it would not be subjected to those great rises and falls that now disconcerts every one. Opdyke in his Political Economy, published in 1851, and from statistics previous to 1846, says : " The natural ratio of money, when expressed in dollars, to population in the United States is as 15 to 1." That country may be considered as a fair standard by which to estimate the quantity of money required by this country ; taking this ratio and our population to be 2,750,000, the Government might issue $41,250,000 of paper money and small change, and by this much reduce the public debt.

Some may consider this a large amount, but to arrive at an approximation of what is necessary, we should take the amount of the deposits and notes in circulation of the banks : calculate the fractional parts of a dollar that are in use, and the amount hoarded by people in the country, (for the hoards are money though not currency) : add these together, and as we are now suffering from the effects of a contraction, make a further allowance to place old debtors on something of a fair footing with their creditors, and this will be the amount that ought to be issued. Were it not for the relation of creditor and debtor, the sum might be fixed at any arbitrary amount, and the value of each portion would soon be determined by competition between the individuals of the community.

In respect to the lowest denomination of the paper currency, half the usual sized note might represent half a dollar, and differently colored twenty cents ; for smaller fractional parts of a dollar some metal had better be used ; tokens of the most durable kind, are the most desirable, and also of the cheapest description, so as to prevent their outflow from the country.

Our employing a money current only in this country will enable foreigners to introduce products so far only as they receive an equivalent from us, all beyond this will be regulated by the wants and wishes of our own people. These wants and wishes on account of our great natural resources will cause the establishment of numberless manufactories throughout the country, and will tax fully the energies of the people.

On account of the full employment of labor, and the healthful nature of our trade, a trade which will enable every industrious man to enjoy the comforts and amenities of life, the immigration into this country, and the natural increase of the population will be so great that if other countries adopt not our principles in their currency, it is probable that in a century or two, this country will become thickly populated. This circumstance may gratify those who attach importance to the having a numerous population ; but this may be deemed of little consequence. The population of this country is already sufficiently great to develope its resources ; to produce an incalculable amount of wealth for their own enjoyment ; and under proper organization to protect that wealth against any foreign interference.

The present banking system during inflations exposes us to excessive importations, which carries away our capital, stops improvements, and bankrupts existing undertakings ; besides it greatly checks enterprise, for cautious people will not incur liabilities, when banks, by a contraction, may at any time double their obligations and reduce them to beggary.

Under the proposed system most things will have a value almost of a fixed nature, and the enterprising man, knowing what he has, can so regulate his proceedings that whenever undertakings prove profitless, he can dispose of his stock, and embark in some other pursuit ; but under the present system oftentimes when a man is carrying on a profitable business, he finds unexpectedly all demand for his goods cease, his debtors unable to pay, no description of property saleable, and to meet his liabilities his property sacrificed for almost nothing. I was told that even the Court of Chancery refused to order the sale of property at a time when things were very much depressed, as forcing a sale amounted to throwing away the property. This state of things cannot arise under a well regulated domestic currency.

The foreigner can compete with our producers only where
for some of our productions he is willing to give more than
what our producers do, but as *machinery* and *skill* advances
in our community, we shall compete with the foreigners till
we arrive at that point which marks distinctly our respective advantages in position, soil and climate. As our powers
of production increase, every one will expect more of his
neighbors goods for his services ; plenty will abound and all
will be in easy circumstances.

Who can predict the results of such a condition ? The
vast increase of educated active brains will continually be
making discoveries and suggesting improvements that will
multiply the productive powers of man to an immeasurable
extent. Every one will so easily enjoy the comforts of life
abundant leisure will be afforded for study and reflection ;
sociology will advance with giant strides ; and the Legislature, in consequence of the independent condition of individuals, will never have to trouble itself with a ten-hour Act,
or with such a measure as lately in England has been
passed in respect to dyers, an account of whose sufferings
astonishes one that such barbarities could ever have been
allowed in a civilized community.

With a domestic currency the trade of the country would
receive such an impetus that its commerce would be alto-
gether subsidiary to it ; and revenue from customs would be
so much affected that recourse would have to be had to other
means for raising revenue, and direct taxation will be the
alternative. This is a far wiser, juster and more economical method than the tariff system ; wiser, as it is far more
simple, and dispenses with great temptations to fraud ;
juster, as men would then bear only their fair proportion of
the taxes ; but under the tariff scheme, when a man indulges
in imported luxuries and fancies he is disproportionably
taxed ; and on what principle of justice or equity is it because
he chooses so to dispose of the fruits of his industry and
labor, that he should bear more than his fair proportion of
the burdens of the State ; and in instances where people
consume little or no foreign productions, they contribute

little or not at all to the general revenue of the country ;
more economical, as the following extract from Opdyke's
Political Economy on the subject demonstrates :—

" We will examine, he says, the practical operation of
each of these methods of raising revenue, and compare their
merits when tested by the principles of equality and economy. Fortunately, we have good data to guide us in the
investigation, since while the General Government practices
the one method, some of the States practice the other. In
the first place, let us see how they compare in point of
economy :

"We pay in custom dues an annual average
of, say... $25,000,000
"We pay to the importer, say 15 per cent.
profit on this sum, for it is well known that
the merchant predicates his profits upon the
whole cost of his goods, upon the duties and
charges, as well as upon the prime cost....... 3,750,000
"We pay the jobbing merchant, say 10 per
cent. profit on these two sums................. 2,875,000
"We pay the retailer, say 25 per cent. on
these three sums............................... 7,906,250

$39,631,250

"We have here an aggregate of $39,531,250 of taxes, paid
by the consumers of foreign goods, of which the Government receives but $25,000,000; and from this sum must be
deducted all the expenses incurred in its collection. These
include, all the rent paid for the use of custom-houses, and
Government warehouses, together with interest on the cost
of those owned by Government; the salaries of the collectors
of customs, and the army of subordinate officers ; and the
expense incident to the marine revenue service. These taken
together cannot be short of $2,500,000 per annum. This
leaves the net receipts of government $22,500,000, which is
little more than half the gross amount contributed ; or to
state the matter more definitely, revenue is collected from

the people by the tariff method at an expense of 77 per cent. on the net amount received by Government. I have purposely excluded from this estimate the immense tribute which these laws compel the consumers of protected domestic products to pay to their producers, because the contrast will be found striking enough without it. But it may be well to state that the Secretary of the Treasury, after an elaborate examination of the question, has estimated the amount of tribute thus paid, under the tariff 1842 at not less than $100,000,-000 annually.

"We find then, that the tariff system of taxation has not the merit of economy to recommend it. Now let us look at the aspect of its proposed substitute, direct taxation. A few years since, the State of New York finding that she needed additional revenue, levied what was called the "Mill Tax;" that is, her citizens were required to contribute one mill of taxes for every dollar of capital or property they possessed. This tax produced an aggregate of $600,000. The assessment and collection of this amount of revenue, cost the State a sum not exceeding $12,000, or two per cent. on the amount collected, which is 75 per cent. cheaper than the tariff method. And there is no obstacle which need prevent the General Government from adopting the same plan. It is perfectly feasible and the transition easy. For example, the same officers who now assess and collect the Township, County and State taxes, in the several States, could assess and collect this also. It could be accomplished without the employment of a single additional officer, and at an expense not exceeding two per cent. In order to secure safety and economy as well as an equitable distribution, the General Government should apportion the tax among the several States, in the ratio of property, or what amounts almost to the same thing, in the ratio of population, and require each State to furnish its quota. The States would as they now do in the management of their own taxes, apportion among their respective Counties, requiring each to furnish its share, and the Counties would apportion it among the Townships. Thus the Federal Government would look to the States, the States to the Counties, the Counties to the Townships, and the Towns to the people, which would give the latter the right of choosing their own assessing and collecting officers.

The system of applying the direct taxation has been adopted by most of the States, and with the happiest results. It has proved to be not only just and economical, but eminently secure, for we rarely hear of a defaulting officer except in large cities; and these appointments are mostly conferred on political partizans of the least scrupulous kind, from such material we could expect no other results.

We find then, that the direct method of taxation is vastly superior to the tariff form of the indirect method, 'not only in point of economy, but equally so as regards security in the process of collection and transmission to the disbursing officers. According to the estimate just presented, the gross cost of collecting our national revenue by the existing method, exceeds $17,000,000 per annum, while that which would attend its collection by the method proposed, would fall short of $500,000, showing a difference in favor of the latter of $16,500,000 per annum. To this sum we may safely add $500,000 for the excess of losses by the former, making the whole difference in favor of the latter, in an economical point of view, not less than $17,000,000 annually. This immense sum the people of the United States would save yearly, in diminished taxation, by the abandonment of tariff laws and the substitution of a judicious system of direct taxation."

To these remarks of Opdyke, I need only add that direct taxation has always been a great bug-bear, yet for municipal purposes we have been long accustomed to it. Why should an extension of the principle be deemed impracticable, especially when under the currency scheme proposed every one can readily obtain the means to pay the taxes Government imposes? In support of these views I may state, that it is only very lately that the Financial Reform Association of England called upon the English Government, on account of its great expensiveness, to abolish all tariff laws and institute direct taxation.

It is objected by some that had we a domestic currency we could not obtain things from abroad. How do we now obtain goods and *gold* from foreign countries? Only by giving something in return. When the present banking system inflates the currency and causes expenditure and extravagance, we exchange our products and gold for commodities; when it contracts, when expenditure receives a great check, we exchange our products for gold only; and thus do we periodically make and lose our capital. A Domestic currency would keep our capital in the country and merchants in the rate of exchange would have a tell-tale by which to regulate their imports and exports.

Besides we have the example of Buenos Ayres and also of Hayti, where a paper currency exists, and though issued in conformity with no established plan, yet these currencies do not prevent their carrying on commerce. In the interior of Hayti people will not take gold when offered them, for they say, it fluctuates in value, which it certainly does, like any other commodity, according to the demand and supply of it for exportation.

A domestic currency established, there will be no bank or banks of issue. The borrowing and lending of money may be left perfectly free to all; but when the money itself does not pass between the parties, but a credit or certificate is given in its stead, the money represented by that credit or certificate, must be set apart, until the presentation of the check or return of the certificate. Whoever practices what McLeod considers "The whole Art and Genius of Banking, which consists in forming a sound judgment as to *how many different parties* he may *pledge the same identical capital.*" Whoever does this! Let him be treated like any other perpetrator of fraud, and be consigned at once to the safe custody of the District Jailor.

The tendencies of the present banking system are eminently demoralizing. By its alternate and ever-recurring expansions and contractions, the measure of value is constantly vibrating. This unsettles business as well as prices;

it makes fortunes and mars them; it excites men's gambling propensities; and oftentimes leads to great extravagance. Under it people are exceedingly jealous and sensitive of their character and reputation, as a breath of suspicion may destroy their prospects for life; the men of commerce stake their interest on the cast of a die; the framework of society is periodically broken up and its energies paralized; it is not possible while such a system exists, but that laborers must be doomed to a life of hard struggle and bondage, and be kept too near a state of absolute want.

It will soon be one of the marvels of the age, that this system has been allowed to prevail so long as it has; for were Sovereigns to tamper with the value of money as do banking corporations at present, the populace could not be restrained from taking the most violent measures to prevent the recurrence of such injustice. But as the action of the banks on money is of a subtle nature and but few understand it, nothing is said; but all suffer, not knowing how or why they do so. So sensible are they on the Spanish Main in South America, of the pernicious influences of of banking institutions, conducted as they now are, that they will not there allow the establishment of a single bank. There is always plenty of money in the country, they say, till a bank is established, and then it becomes so scarce few can obtain it. The same phenomenon has been noticed in Jamaica.

A domestic currency would cause the people of the country to regard each other's wants rather than those of foreigners, and thus save them the great losses that distant voyages and management occasion. It would afford a much more effectual protection to the industry of the country than high duties, which present but poor barriers when an inflation of the currency takes place, and which, besides, are now generally conceded as unjust to consumers.

THE SUPERIORITY OF MONEY OVER BANK-DEBT IN THE CURRENCY.

With money we buy property and pay for it, and the money then remains keeping the currency whole to maintain prices and discharge all obligations contracted by its measure; with the debt-currency we buy property by transferring a debt; we pass an order on the bank; the bank then owes for the property instead of ourselves, and promises to pay money hereafter. I owe $1,000 to Johnstone, $1,000 of money will pay and end the debt, leaving the currency entire. Not having the money I give him an order on the bank. The bank now owes Johnstone what I owed him before; the debt is not paid. If the bank discharges its debt by an off-set with its creditor, it annihilates so much of the currency. This is simply the contraction of bank-loans; it is an absolute destruction of the means of paying the obligations it had created in the price of things; the price must fall. This is the important difference between money and debt in the currency. Money remains to support prices and maintain the integrity of obligations, after paying and ending debt. The debt currency cannot pay and end debt without destroying the sum of the currency. See the wretched effect of this in an illustration.

A trader by industry and frugality acquires $10,000 clear balance at the credit of his stock account with a certain increase of currency. His assets are $30,000 and he owes $20,000. This is an average position of traders in the country. Now the banks being obliged to pay their debts annihilate so much of this currency, as was really the case in the fall of 1857, that general prices fall one-half. The trader's debtors cannot pay, his merchandise falls, and his assets fall one-half; he has $20,000 to pay and only $15,000 left to pay it with. Instead of being worth $10,000 he is now bankrupt $5,000 without any imprudence or fault of his own, but simply by the miserable instability of this principle of debt in the currency. The reader no doubt knows many cases of this sort occurring in the fall of 1857. One occurred where a merchant, worth nearly $200,000, owed less than the half of his net estate,—a prudent, exemplary man and an indefatigable worker, he was ruined and is now in an insane asylum.

We see by this example that it requires the whole sum of the currency to discharge the obligations contracted by its measure. We cannot fall back on the money portion of the currency to supply the deficiencies of the other, because the money is employed in its own functions, in effecting the exchanges depending upon it. No matter how much money may remain in the currency the debtor can have no means to obtain it, when his means depend upon prices that have fallen.

For convenience sake the payment for commodities passes through the medium of the currency, and the *promise* of the currency being *to pay dollars*, (and not land, public stock, or private indebtedness,) nothing else will meet that promise when dollars are demanded.

There are other facts of great significance. A high rate of interest indicates the abnormal condition of the currency shewing the preponderance of debt in relation to the money it contains. Debt in the currency has more effect in raising the rate of interest than debt anywhere else. By driving money away it increases the demand for it. As the debt currency increases the rate of interest rises, and, except in the frenzy of the change, as it decreases, the rate of interest falls; a guarantee for the risk of bad debts, inseparable from the debt currency system, is always included in the rate of interest.

The sales on credit are made with a charge included for guarantee against bad debts, which with a money currency would be saved. It is believed that commodities pass on the average through five persons on their way from producers to consumers, with an average charge of four per cent. in each sale to cover the abnormal risk, so that articles reach consumers with an extra and unnecessary cost of twenty per cent. This falls on the producers in two ways, it checks their production and sales, and compels them to feed and clothe great numbers without their knowledge and consent. Obviously the evil cannot be removed while debt remains in the currency.

There can be no objection to the credit system either in the ordinary traffic of the country, or in banking. *Credit banking* is a very different thing from *debt banking*. Banks should employ their credit to obtain money, and then loan it to the best advantage. They should borrow and lend money as individuals borrow and lend money. Debt banking; the system of the Bank of England, costs this country an immense amount of money, and an untold amount of wretchedness in the dissipation of the hard-earned fortunes of worthy and industrious men. It subjects the wealth of the country to all the hazard of a game of chance. The remedy lies in honest unequivocal *money* banking.

Mr. Fullerton is the chief modern authority for the notion so prevalent in England and in this country, that all public financial difficulties spring from overtrading, the banks being perfectly innocent and uninfluential in the matter,—" The amount of issues," he says, " of the country banks is exclusively regulated by the extent of local dealing and expenditure in their respective districts, fluctuating with the fluctuation of production and price, and they neither can increase their issues beyond the limits which the range of such dealing and expenditure prescribes ; nor diminish them, but at an almost equal certainty of the currency being filled up from some other source."

If $10,000,000 of gold were thrown upon the Canadian market to-day, in excess of the present supply, it would unquestionably cause an immediate and material decline in the local value of money here ; there would be much " local dealing and expenditure ;" prices would rise, and imports would be attracted by the high prices until that excess of money could be distributed to an equation of value with other places. It would ultimately find its level of value over the whole commercial world.

Precisely the same result as to the decline in value and distribution in money would follow the precipitation of the same amount of convertible bank currency upon the market. Let it be known that the banks are prepared to furnish $10,000,000 by discounts in addition to the present local volume of currency, and a ruinously active business would take place in the creation of notes for discount; competition in prices; and in imports from other places, to be held at high prices, by means of bank accommodations. There would be plenty of speculation, which would be of no use whatever in approximating goods to the consumer, but only a ruinous tax upon their necessary consumption; this would continue until the banks were checked in their destructive course.

The experience of 1857 and the preceding years, like other periods of great changes in the volume of the currency and value of money, clearly disprove the doctrine of Mr. Fullerton. How was it also in France under the operation of Law's bank from 1716 to 1720? There can be no doubt that the local dealing and expenditure kept pace with the operations of the bank; there was prodigious activity for a while, and a prodigious advance of general prices. Mr. Fullerton would make the mad speculations of that period the cause of the bank issues, and such has been the argument of all the Bank-paper currency advocates in every commercial revulsion in England and this country. It surely will not answer, they mistake effect for cause.

If Mr. Fullerton's theory were correct the converse would also be true, but does the decline of "local dealing and expenditure" cause the contraction of bank loans? or is it the contraction of bank loans which causes the decline of the local dealing and expenditure?

When banks deal in money only, there is no need of *liabilities* without *money in reserve* against them. With this reserve the loans are released from all restraint, and money, like every thing else, may be left to the natural law of supply and demand.

The following *pro forma* account may serve to illustrate this method of banking.

$1,000,000 proprietors' capital paid in money.
5,000,000 deposits on stipulated terms, or with due notice
─────── of withdrawal.
$6,000,000

Loan at discount and in exchange dealings, say
7 per cent. per annum.............................. $420,000

Contra.

Interest on $5,000,000 deposits at 5 per
  annum.................................... $250,000
Loss of interest on $40,000 money in re-
  serve at 7 per cent..................... 2,800
Rent $1,500 ; salaries $9,000............ 10,500
Bad debts one-fifth of 1 per cent., say... 12,000
Contingencies.............................. 4,700
                         ─────── $280,000

Dividend on proprietors' capital 14 per
  cent. per annum...................... $140,000

The loan must be so averaged as to time, that the receipts shall always preceed the demand for payment of the deposits. The operation of the Saving Banks, without any capital at all, shew that large deposits may be obtained. With such ample capital as above stated, to protect and give entire confidence to depositors, or with less capital deposits of less amount may be maintained at five times the amount of the capital. The loans should be made on commercial paper and active securities so that the money would be constantly employed in the currency, either in money or in checks, or certificates of deposit, with money in reserve, dollar for dollar, against the liabilities. Such reserve would be a special deposit without interest. This institution would be an honest "money bank," dealing in capital, getting money before loaning it.

Our bankers assert that such is the nature of the business of this country, that expansions and contractions of the currency are necessary. In the fall of the year, they say, the produce cannot be brought out of the country for exportation, unless the currency is increased. As soon as the bills drawn for these exports are sold, then a contraction ensues. So much has already been said on the evils of expansions and contractions, I need not dwell on the mischievousness of this proceeding. The same end would be attained by banks offering a sufficiently high rate of interest to draw money from sources, where it was lying idle, or where it could not be so profitably employed.

It is contended that the establishment of a domestic currency, regulated as proposed, will not prevent expansions and contractions; that the currency will circulate in other countries and as the amount that will do so will vary, by so much will expansions and contractions take place. I believe though of some value, yet it will be of such uncertain value abroad that this currency will never there enter into circulation. I will first suppose that we alone possess a domestic currency, and that other nations continue the use of metals for their money; the natural relative value of our money may be higher, or may be less than theirs, the value of each depending on its relation to services in the respective countries; our dollar here may command twice or only half the amount of services that the gold dollar does in other countries. Next, I will suppose that other countries adopt domestic currencies; the natural relative value of theirs and ours will be almost sure to differ; besides, did a difference in their natural relative value not exist, we may be certain that the exchanges between the countries would always be causing one money to be more valuable than another. For these reasons we may be assured that this currency abroad will never enter into general circulation, not even near our borders, where the paper of our banks freely circulates.

It is also contended that expansions and contractions will most probably arise by parties combining and withdrawing large sums from circulation to serve purposes of their own. A domestic currency will cause wealth to be so much more fairly distributed than it has ever yet been done, that this will be no easy matter to accomplish ; but, suppose that it were accomplished, as it is the duty of the Government to jealously guard the measure of value, as soon as they detect great appreciation in the currency and can trace it to such causes, they should at once be empowered to counteract such action by a further issue of notes ; and when the hoarded sum was released to withdraw the extra issue, which would then become a public debt. The fear of such a power being exercised, I have very little doubt, would be sufficient to deter the formation of any such combinations. Against the *possibility* of their arising, the only weakness in the scheme proposed, (for to prevent any abuse in the issues I cannot regard as one,) and which can be remedied, we have the *damning realities* of the present banking system.

The employment of bank-debt has the effect of expelling and repelling money which would otherwise be employed in the place of the abnormal, useless, and bewildering bank-debt. Its contraction reduces the money value of the assets of debtors, and does not reduce the sum of their obligations, and creditors gain the property that is lost by debtors, in consequence of the contraction.

The measures best calculated to redress these evils, as well as to greatly stimulate the industry of the country are, the establishment of a currency based on public faith, on public laws, regulated in amount, and valueless out of the country, and the no further legalizing the fraudulent transactions of banks. A wharfinger or merchant, who pledges the same goods twice, is treated as a swindler ; and banks also ought to be treated as perpetrators of fraud whenever they pledge more than once the same money.

These measures would approximate the producer and consumer, it would draw together the population of the country ; and not disperse it as the present monetary and banking systems do. With the removal of all restrictions on interchanges with foreigners, the measures proposed, would give rise to a continuously progressive condition, till it raised this country from its present condition, to one of great prosperity and wealth.

To hasten the advent of such a condition, the Government should, to the utmost, promote and diffuse knowledge; and forward facilities of communication between different parts of the country; it need not concern itself with canal or railroad routes, for merely through traffic or travel's sake, for if these undertakings will pay, they may safely be left to private enterprise, and if they will not, Government should not for the convenience of people beyond our borders enter into such profitless undertakings.

No apprehension need be entertained respecting the ability of Government to put treasury notes into circulation. When prepared to issue them, let an act be passed rendering null and void all notes of the banks not presented for payment within three or six months; making the treasury notes the only legal tender; enabling banks to redeem their liabilities with them; and making it criminal to pledge the same money more than once. Then let Government issue its notes, undertaking to receive them and *them only* in payment of all dues to itself, to any one on receiving value, or to any one on giving security for the amount advanced, and willing to pay interest for the same.

PROTECTION.

Since the currency any one possesses is evidence of services due to him, it is evident that when he requires some of these services to be rendered to him, the arrangement of the price, or the value of the service, should be left entirely to the natural agreement of the buyer and seller. Who can tell so well as they what is the real value of the service? Now, suppose that when the price of the service was so agreed upon and settled between the parties, some artificial force were suddenly put into the power of either of them, beyond what arose from their natural position, to enable one of them to compel the other to yield up more of his industry than he ought to do; such a force suddenly put into the hands of either party, whatever its nature be, whether moral or material, would clearly be unjust in its very nature, and it would be nothing more than a force enabling one party to rob the other.

It is the Divine command, that man should live by his industry, and he has been endowed with power and faculties to enable him to fulfil that command. A man's industry therefore, and the fruits of that industry, are his sacred possession, bestowed upon him by the Divine Author and Governor of the world. It may therefore be asserted in the broadest possible terms, that it is the natural right of every man to employ his industry and the talents which Providence has given him, in a manner which he considers the most advantageous to himself, as long as it is not to the injury of his neighbor. He has a natural right to exchange the products of his own industry, with those of any other person who will agree to do it, to buy from whom he will, and to sell to whom he can. Any law which seeks to check the cause of this free exchange is inherently wrong, and though it may be permitted to take something from him for the necessities of the State, a law which seeks to despoil one class of the community of the fruits of their industry and give them to another is an intolerable violation of natural justice.

Now, the primary idea which lies at the foundation of all property is industry; and if a man takes away any portion of another man's property, it may be considered as so much of his industry. Thus if he wishes to sell any article to him and purchase gold with it, if he can by any means whatever force him to pay a higher price for it than he otherwise would; it is simply despoiling him of part of his industry, and appropriating it to himself.

Let us put this in a familiar way. Suppose Richard Stubble lives in the country and is a corn grower, and his friend John Smith carries on his business in town, and has accumulated money by his frugality and industry. Having some corn to sell, Richard proposes to have a transaction with his friend John. The free marketable value of the corn is $100 per 100 bushels; but suppose that Richard has about one hundred times as much influence over the legislature that John has, and he gets them to make a law by which he can compel John to pay him $120 for what he could get elsewhere for $100. That is, he takes away $20, representing so much of John's industry, from him against his will, for which he gives him no equivalent and takes it to himself. In the mediæval ages great lords and barons used to keep armed retainers, whom they employed to plunder any unfortunate travellers who came within their power. In the 19th century great lords and gentlemen passed a law by which they forced traders to surrender to them a considerable portion of their property against their will. Where is the moral difference between the two cases? When one man forcibly and unjustly deprives another of his property, the precise method he may adopt for attaining his purpose does not affect the moral aspect of the thing.

It is no argument whatever to say that the protective system was till lately established in England, and is still in force in foreign countries, nor that it was supported and adopted by men of unblemished character and integrity. It is absolutely necessary that we should not suffer our estimation of the moral character of men to influence our judgment as to the soundness of their opinions. There scarcely ever prevailed a pernicious error in the world, which was not supported by the authority of men of eminent personal excellence. The real question is not whether the men who hold certain opinions are estimable, but whether the opinions themselves are right or wrong. Few persons are either so good or so bad as their opinions. The fact is, that questions are examined with far greater intelligence and care now-a-days than ever they were before, and by the more comprehensive investigation, new considerations and relations are discovered, which may present them in very different lights than are apparent at first. Abstract right is every day obtaining a greater influence in legislation, and many of the most striking and beneficial reforms of the present day have been to abolish and set aside the partial and unjust laws which encumbered the Statute-book. It is not so very long ago that public opinion in this country tolerated, and men of eminent piety saw no harm in the Slave Trade, in stealing men from their homes and transferring them to foreign countries to labor for the benefit of their masters. But public opinion became convinced of its abomination, and not only put it down, but declared it to be a great crime. What was considered to be legitimate traffic fifty years ago, is now declared by law to be piracy, and Englishmen who engage in it are liable to be dealt with as pirates. Now, there is not at bottom much difference in the idea involved in Protection and the Slave Trade. They both seek to effect the same object by somewhat different methods. They are both for the purpose of enabling one set of men to appropriate to themselves the fruits of their neighbours' industry—the one by the coarser method of force the other by the more refined system of fraud. Lord Macaulay remarks, " that the two greatest, and most salutary social revolutions which have taken place in England were those which, in the 13th centuary put an end to the tyrrany of nation over nation, and that which a few years later, put an end to the property of man in man." To these we may venture to add a *third*, not less great, and not less salutary than the other two—the great revolution in the minds of the age, which, in the 19th century abolished for ever the property of one set of men *in the industry* of others.

The protective system is, therefore, nothing more than a measure by which producers endeavour to force consumers to pay a higher price than they otherwise would for the same commodities. Now let us consider a somewhat different case.

Suppose that the Legislature, being entirely composed of consumers, should pass a law forbidding the farmers to sell their produce above a certain price, or to export it to foreign countries, where they might find a better market for it. Or suppose laws had been passed to prevent workmen from demanding above a certain rate of wages, or compelling producers to bring their productions to market, and accept a price for them much below what they would fetch if there were no such law. This would be a case on the part of the consumers precisely analogous to what protection is on the part of producers.

This form of economic error never was sufficiently prevalent in England to require a distinctive name in our language, but it did in France. During the height of the French Revolution in 1793, when the insecurity of property had scared away almost all sorts of produce from the market, the French Convention passed the severest laws to limit the price of commodities, forbidding persons to sell their produce above certain fixed prices whence these laws were called the laws of the Maximum. As might have been foreseen, these laws only aggravated the evil; and their disastrous effects are set forth with great minuteness in the third, fourth, fifth, and sixth volumes of Alison's History of Europe, (7th ed.) though the author overlooks the fact that the very same objections apply against the system of protection of which he is so strong an advocate.

Each of these systems then, is erroneous, but in opposite direction; that of protection by which the producer obliges the consumer to buy from him his produce at a price above its intrinsic value, that of the maximum, by which the producer is obliged to sell his produce to the consumer, at a price below its marketable value. Now, every law whatever that interferes with the natural course of trade, which attempts to regulate the wages of labor, or the price of commodities, which attempts to meddle with the free exchange of industry between man and man, must necessarily fall under one of these forms of error. Every such law sins against natural justice, more or less, in one direction or the other, and is an aggression of one party on the other, either as it assumes the form of protection or the maximum ; and it is just as clear as the sun at noon-day, that the only true, just and proper course, is to leave things to find their own level, or in other words, to establish and maintain absolute freedom of trade. Now, the idea that was at the foundation of all this legislation, was, that the cost of production should govern price, and that persons who produce articles, had a right to have remunerative prices secured to them by law. This idea was a very natural one to occur to producers, and when we think of the condition of Parliament, at the time when this species of legislation was in fashion, we shall not be surprised at its having prevailed. In the last century it is true, there were at various times laws enacted for the purpose of disturbing the natural course of trade, but the corn laws which lasted with various alterations till Sir R. Peel so happily abolished them, were made in 1815. Now, what was the state of Parliament at that time ? One branch was entirely composed, as it still is, of agriculturists ; the other principally of agriculturists and the nominees of agriculturists, as well as great merchants, great ship owners, and great producers of all sorts. It was entirely a Parliament of Sellers—a vast, close and corrupt combination. The great body of the people, that is the consumers, had scarcely any influence whatever in the House of Commons. The sellers had a complete monopoly of law making, and their legislation was exactly what might have been expected. All the producers in turn were permitted to plunder the public for their own benefit. It was nothing more than a gigantic conspiracy of all the Sellers against all the Buyers.

www.ingramcontent.com/pod-product-compliance
Lightning Source LLC
Chambersburg PA
CBHW021644270326
41931CB00008B/1169